I0796119

PRACTICAL CAREERS FOR PRACTICAL PEOPLE

ELECTRICIAN

Cathleen Small

Published in 2026 by **Cheriton Children's Books**
1 Bank Drive West, Shrewsbury, Shropshire, SY3 9DJ, UK

First Edition

Author: Cathleen Small
Designer: Jessica Moon
Editor: Sarah Eason
Proofreader: Ella Short

Picture credits: Cover: Shutterstock/NT Studio. Inside: p4: Shutterstock/Dmitry Kalinovsky, p5: Shutterstock/Amorn Suriyan, p6: Shutterstock/Pakulin Sergei, p7: Shutterstock/Shutter.B, p9b: Shutterstock/Carlos Barquero, p9t: Shutterstock/Hryshchyshen Serhii, p10: Shutterstock/Everett Collection, p11: Shutterstock/M2020, p12: Shutterstock/PV Productions, p13: Shutterstock/Amorn Suriyan, p14: Shutterstock/Monkey Business Images, p15: Shutterstock/Alpa Prod, p16: Shutterstock/Fizkes, p17: Shutterstock/Dizain, p18: Shutterstock/PhotoByToR, p19: Shutterstock/Andrey Popov, p20: Shutterstock/Air Images, p21: Shutterstock/Monkey Business Images, p22: Shutterstock/Monkey Business Images, p23: Shutterstock/Skipper SR, p24: Shutterstock/VG Foto, p25: Shutterstock/Alpa Prod, p26: Shutterstock/Atelier211, p27: Shutterstock/Png Studio Photography, p28: Shutterstock/Ball Lunla, p30: Shutterstock/Oo3asy6Olfoo, p31: Shutterstock/Kaninw, p32: Shutterstock/Phovoir, p33: Shutterstock/Usoltsev Kirill, p34l: Shutterstock/DC Studio, p34r: Shutterstock/Andrew Angelov, p36: Shutterstock/NT Studio, p37: Shutterstock/PV Productions, p38: Shutterstock/Maroke, p39: Shutterstock/Ira Lichi, p40: Wikimedia Commons, p41: Shutterstock/Comeo/Frederic Legrand, p42: Shutterstock/SeventyFour, p43: Shutterstock/Krakenimages.com, p44: Shutterstock/Worradirek, p46b: Shutterstock/Kardasov Films, p46t: Shutterstock/Trek6500, p48: Shutterstock/Zula Albab, p50: Shutterstock/Amorn Suriyan, p51: Shutterstock/Hryshchyshen Serhii, p52: Shutterstock/Narai Chal, p53: Shutterstock/Franco Lucato, p55l: Shutterstock/1st Footage, p55r: Shutterstock/Kittirat Roekburi, p56l: Shutterstock/Worradirek, p56r: Shutterstock/Minerva Studio, p63: Shutterstock/Alpa Prod.

Printed in China

CONTENTS

CHAPTER 1

Working in the Electrical Industry

Many students look forward to the day they graduate high school and head off to college. But not all students. For some, college holds little appeal. Perhaps they aren't interested in taking on the financial burden of higher education. They may not be interested in at least four more years of study. They simply may prefer working with their hands over doing the "desk" type of job that many graduates land. If that sounds like you, we've got good news! There's a wealth of careers for people who like jobs that involve working with their hands.

There is great potential to build a strong future career in the trades, and that's partly due to a lack of skilled workers in this area.

GOOD NEWS FOR PRACTICAL PEOPLE

In fact, there's a great demand for skilled workers in the trades. That's because the workforce in those jobs has been aging, and many tradespeople are now retiring. Years ago, it was common for people to pursue a practical career, such as in construction, plumbing, electrical work, or another

With the rise of energy efficiency goals, there's no better time to consider a career in the electrical field for men and women interested in the trades.

similar trade. Sure, some people went to college and worked office jobs, but many chose a career in a more practical line of work.

Somewhere along the way, that dynamic shifted, with many people instead pursuing college degrees and the associated career paths. The people working in the trades still worked in them, of course. However, there weren't nearly as many new people entering those fields. And so, as many tradespeople are now retiring, a huge labor shortage in the trades has resulted. National Public Radio (NPR) reported that in recent years, the application rates for trade jobs such as electrician and plumber dropped by 49 percent. And in 2024, the construction industry reported it needed an astounding half a million additional workers.

All this is great news if you're interested in a practical career. You're needed! And electrical work is an excellent field to enter, in part because of the labor shortage in this particular employment sector.

WORKING IN THE ELECTRICAL INDUSTRY

Another reason why the electrical field is a growing job market is all the new technologies that seem to arrive daily. Electricians who are trained to use them are needed. Consider one of the latest important innovations: energy-efficient products. Many of them are electrical. Renewable energy sources such as solar and wind are great, but how do we use that energy? We convert it into electricity. And then electricians are needed to work with that resulting power. For example, when people put solar panels on their homes to attempt to harness the power of the sun for energy, they often need to upgrade their electrical panels. And who does that? Electricians.

We'll talk about more technologies and jobs that require electricians later in this book. But the takeaway at this point is there's a great need for electricians, and because of that, it's an excellent career choice for practical people to consider.

IMPORTANT POINTS TO THINK ABOUT

When you're thinking about your future career as an electrician, there are several important factors to carefully consider:

- Do you have skills in the electrical field, or could you develop them?
- Will the job be secure?
- Will the job likely exist in the future as technology advances and introduces changes to the workplace?
- What is the pay?
- What training is involved, and how much will it cost?
- What benefits does the electrical field offer in addition to pay?

We'll explore the answers to all the above questions in this chapter.

IN IT FOR THE LONG TERM

Currently, across genders and states, the average retirement age for American citizens is 64. This means that people of your generation will likely be working for a significant amount of time. So it's important to choose your career carefully—you will probably be doing it for many years to come.

THINKING AHEAD

You've probably just begun to think seriously about your career. And you've probably realized that you'll likely be working for at least 40 years, depending on when you retire. That means your career should be something you enjoy. Naturally, you can change careers later in life if you decide you don't like what you're doing. But making big changes to your work can be difficult as you get older, so it's good to explore career options now, when you have some time to narrow down what you think you would enjoy doing as a career for the coming decades.

Lineman is just one job in the electrical industry that might appeal to you. If you're not afraid of heights and you enjoy working outdoors, this might be an area to consider.

With so much new technology underway, the electrical field is an exciting area to work in.

WOULD YOU ENJOY BEING AN ELECTRICIAN?

So let's talk about whether you'd like being an electrician. One real benefit to being an electrician is the variety of work in your job. There is a host of things that can go wrong in an electrical system, so it's likely that no two days will look the same. Sure, you might spend a good chunk of time on one task. For example, you might put in place new electrical panels for people installing solar. But unless you're working on a new home development, no two houses are likely to be wired in the same way. That means unforeseen issues can crop up anywhere.

In this job, you'll likely be meeting different customers, which keeps life interesting. You may work in people's homes and workplaces, which means you will get to meet a lot of individuals. And if you don't particularly enjoy meeting people, there are still many jobs within the electrical industry in which you're less likely to be working face-to-face with a lot of customers.

CHANGING WORK ENVIRONMENT

"As an electrician, you are working in different places all the time. That helps make the job interesting. I like waking up in the morning and knowing I'll be going somewhere new."

OTHER ADVANTAGES

If you work in people's homes, you'll likely be appreciated. Electrical work is daunting for people who aren't trained in it, and homeowners are generally happy to have a skilled tradesperson come to their home to fix or improve it.

For people who would like to be self-employed, there are many opportunities to work independently as an electrician. You can work for an established company, but you can also set up your own electrician service and be your own boss, if you prefer.

And finally, electricians make good money. It's a skilled trade in high demand, and the pay shows that.

DO YOU HAVE THE RIGHT SKILLS?

Maybe you're interested in electricity because it's a strong career field with the potential for good pay. Maybe you're interested because your parent was an electrician and taught you the basics when you were young. Or maybe you just really liked to play with snap circuits as a kid. Either way, you may have the skills to be an electrician.

Many of the skills you need to be a good electrician are transferable from other areas. For example, snap circuits teach the basics of how electricity moves from one

BENJAMIN FRANKLIN'S LIGHTNING MOMENT

Benjamin Franklin may be best known as one of America's Founding Fathers, but he is also well known for his discoveries about how electricity can be harnessed. He theorized that lightning was in fact electricity, and he used his famous experiment of tying a key to a kite string to capture the electricity from lightning to prove his point. In his work with electricity, Franklin used several terms that we still use today to talk about electricity, including:

- Battery
- Charge
- Conductor
- Positive
- Plus
- Minus
- Negative

It's a myth that Franklin discovered electricity, since one can't really discover something that has been a part of people's lives since the beginning of time. (We've always had lightning!) However, Franklin discovered that we could capture it from sources and use it.

Some people in the electrical industry enjoy putting on the finishing touches, such as installing lighting fixtures and switches in homes.

area to another based on a series of connections. Math skills are important for electricians, so all the math homework you've done in school will help your career as an electrician. Are you good at looking at schematics for how to build things and then putting those things together based on the design? Then you've got some useful skills that will be helpful when looking at blueprints.

Does that mean you're ready to jump into a career in the electrical industry? Not yet. But it does mean you have a start on developing the skills you'll need to do the job.

If you think you might enjoy working in the electrical field, it's never too early to start taking some classes or tinkering with circuits.

IS THERE JOB SECURITY?

Job security is an important consideration when planning your future career. You want to choose a career that will still be going strong in 20, 30, or even 40 years. The good news is the outlook for electricians is strong. According to the Bureau of Labor Statistics (BLS), job growth for electricians is expected to be 6 percent over the next decade. That's double the expected growth rate for all jobs in the United States! In other words, there is true job security if you're a skilled electrician.

EARNING POTENTIAL

"Salaries are important, and you can earn a decent one as an electrician. You'll earn more than the national average wage. It's a skilled job, and the pay reflects that."

SUCCESS STORIES

Thomas Edison is well known for his life as a great inventor. One of his inventions was the incandescent light bulb. Light bulbs had been created earlier (before Edison was even born), but Edison discovered that a filament of carbonized thread was needed to create a long-lasting incandescent light bulb that could be used in homes. Under Edison's company, the first commercial electric light system in the country was installed in Lower Manhattan, featuring 400 lamps!

One important fact about Edison is that while he is credited for many amazing ideas, he had many failures as well. When asked about these failures, Edison famously said, "I have not failed 10,000 times—I've successfully found 10,000 ways that will not work." Wise words to put in perspective that failure doesn't have to be a negative—it can instead be a stepping stone to success.

Thomas Edison turned failures into success by seeing each one as a chance to understand why things do or do not work.

Electricians trained to use the newest technology should have plenty of job opportunities.

Technology continues to develop, and the need for skilled electricians continues to grow alongside that development. Unlike some other professions, in which technological growth is costing skilled workers their jobs, the electrical industry should continue to respond well to developing technology.

WHAT WILL THE FUTURE BRING?

Today, many people believe that there is a looming threat or benefit in all industries, depending on how you view it. It is artificial intelligence (AI). There are fears that AI and robots will replace human workers, costing people jobs. Some worry that AI will spell the end of the American workforce as we know it, while others embrace AI and look forward to seeing where the technology will take us.

In the electrical industry, AI is being used as a tool to help electricians, and is shifting some electrical work from a repair model to a maintenance model. That is, AI tools are predicting issues with electrical systems. They can then be addressed by an electrician carrying out maintenance.

There are certainly some aspects of electrical work that will likely be impacted by AI and robots. But people who embrace the fact that AI is here to stay and learn how to use it intelligently in their own work are likely to remain in demand.

INTERESTING WORK

"I never get bored in my job. When you're an electrician, you get to work on a lot of different jobs. No two days are the same. If you like variety, it's a great job."

Physical fitness is a must for this job, and good hand-eye coordination will help you make fine adjustments that are sometimes needed.

IS IT THE RIGHT JOB FOR YOU?

So is being an electrician the right job for you? There are certain skills and abilities you'll need to have if you want to succeed in this field.

First, are you a good problem-solver? While AI is shifting some electrical work from a repair model to a maintenance model, there is still a need for electricians to be able to problem-solve. AI is far from all-knowing, and sometimes there is no replacement for a human when it comes to problem-solving. AI relies on searching the Internet to find information about what has been done before. However, to problem-solve you need critical-thinking skills, and that's where AI fails. AI cannot think critically. It can only collect data on similar issues and give a response. If you can look at a problem and think critically about how to solve it, you're ahead of AI.

PHYSICAL FITNESS AND SUITABILITY

Are you physically fit? Electrical work involves a certain amount of manual labor and, sometimes, heavy lifting, so you'll need to be strong and fit to carry out that work.

Do you have good manual dexterity (which means you are nimble with your fingers and thumbs), and do you have good hand-eye coordination? Electricians work with often-delicate wires, and that type of work requires dexterity along with good hand-eye coordination.

A PEOPLE PERSON?

Are you good with people? Many electricians work directly with customers, so good people skills are a must! Even those who have less customer-facing jobs need a certain level of people-skills. They may work with other tradespeople on the same project or with local officials on inspections and other tasks. Your skill at working with electrical components is most important, but people skills are very important as well.

Are you a good communicator? Electrical work is complicated and often not easily understood by many people. You may need to communicate information about complex topics in a way that is understandable to the average homeowner or building manager.

TIME MANAGEMENT

Have you thought about your time-management skills? Time is money, as they say, and that is true in the electrical world. Often, you need to be able to estimate how long a job will take, and then complete it in that amount of time so you can get to the next job. Also, if you're part of the construction team for a building project, you need to do your part efficiently so the next members of the team can get to their work.

READING PLANS AND LEARNING

How are you at reading schematics and are you open to learning new things? Electricians often need to consult blueprints to construct and/or repair electrical systems. Building codes and regulations change, and you'll need to keep up on the latest ones in your work as an electrician. Electricians need to keep learning and changing their practice to keep up to speed with new technology.

The technology in electricity is changing all the time. Electricians must keep up with these changes to do their job.

HOW MUCH WILL I EARN?

Hopefully, a career in the electrical industry sounds appealing to you based on what you've learned so far. The next issue to look at is pay. Here are the key facts about pay for electricians. On average, the median income for electricians is around $61,500. The top 10 percent, however, earn more than $100,000.

Pay depends on many factors, including experience, who you work for, and where you work. An electrician in a tiny town in a sparsely populated area, for example, is likely to earn less than an electrician in a high-priced city such as New York or Chicago.

In fact, websites such as Salary.com, Glassdoor.com, and ZipRecruiter.com report that the average salary for electricians in New York City is anywhere from just under $70,000 per year to above $100,000 per year—all certainly above the median income. Experience is key, too. An apprentice electrician makes less than a journeyman electrician. Both make less than a master electrician.

So keep all these facts in mind when you think about your future earnings. Salary for an experienced electrician is strong. However, the pay is ultimately determined by where you live, who you work for, and your skills and training.

Electricians are trained in simulation settings so that they are well versed in dealing with many practical problems once they enter the workplace.

LOOKING AT SALARIES AND COSTS OF COLLEGE

As you've learned, the salary for electricians is fairly strong. One thing that is also helpful in choosing your career path is weighing the salary expectations for electrical work against the cost of going to college. Electrical work doesn't require a four-year college degree (unless you want to become a fully-fledged electrical engineer). Instead, there are several training paths you can follow, but none of them is as expensive as going to college for a degree. You can attend a trade school or you can attend community college. You can also explore apprenticeship options. Either way, the cost of your training will be far less than the cost of a four-year degree.

The Education Data Initiative (EDI) reports that the average cost of a four-year college education at an in-state public university in the United States in 2024 was more than $108,000. At an out-of-state university, that cost rose to more than $182,000. At a private university, that cost jumped to more than $234,000. The Initiative also notes that the average borrower of student loans spends about 20 years paying them off.

The cost of electrical schools varies widely but tends to be anywhere from $1,000 to about $20,000, depending on where you go. Even at the top end of that range, the cost is still far less than what you would pay for four years at college. In some cases, it is far less than you'd pay for even just one year of college.

Trade school and community college cost a fraction of the price of a university degree, and apprenticeships are free of charge.

WHICH WAY TO GO?

If you opt for the community college route, tuition costs vary widely based on where you live. However, it's less than the cost of four years at university, and some states offer free community college to residents for a set period, such as the first year. The EDI reported that the average cost of in-district community college in 2024 was just over $4,000. The cost of education is an important factor. Spending six figures on a college education is sensible if you have a career plan that requires you to have a four-year degree, or more. But if a practical career such as being an electrician is more interesting to you, then a major plus is that you won't have to build up a lot of debt to accomplish your schooling. Less debt means more of your hard-earned money stays in your pocket. (We'll discuss training in further detail in Chapter 2.)

Factoring in the different costs of training is part of the equation in choosing the right path for you.

Compensations and Benefits

Benefits, in particular, make up a big part of your total compensation package.

OTHER BENEFITS

Pay is important, but how much you earn isn't everything. You should also consider the total compensation package that comes with a job. Total compensation typically includes your salary, any insurance offerings (such as health and life), and any retirement plans.

What your total compensation package includes depends very much on your employer and whether you are self-employed or employed by a company. If you're self-employed, you must acquire your own insurance and set up your own retirement plan. If you're employed by a company, your employer may or may not provide these. Either way, electricians can join a union and can generally set up insurance and retirement plans through the union. (We'll discuss unions in more detail in Chapter 2.)

LET'S TALK ABOUT TAXES

If you're hired by a company as a regular employee, they'll take taxes out of your paycheck. But as an electrician, you may be self-employed or employed as a contractor. On the surface, that looks like you get a higher paycheck—and indeed you often do. However, that's because your employer doesn't have to pay for insurance or taxes for you—rather, you pay for those yourself. Along with paying the state and federal taxes that an employer typically takes out, you also must pay a 15.3 percent self-employment tax that goes toward covering what an employer would have paid into Medicare and Social Security for you. That 15.3 percent isn't a small amount, so you'll want to consider that when you think about the type of electrician job you ultimately want to get.

INSURANCE: AN IMPORTANT CONSIDERATION

Electrical work isn't particularly dangerous, but accidents can happen, and if they do you'll want to make sure you have good insurance coverage.

You may not yet have thought about insurance. It may seem very grown up, and perhaps a little boring! After all, thinking about what your dream job will be like is far more exciting. However, once you enter the world of work, protection becomes very important. Insurance is an important part of working as an electrician, and several types of insurance need to be considered. We'll discuss them on these two pages.

IMPORTANT FOR EVERYONE

Health and life insurance are important for everyone. Health insurance covers you when you need to see a doctor—and medical debt can be so enormous that it can bankrupt people, so you don't want to go without insurance. While health insurance can be expensive, it is worth it if you need to see a doctor or have a hospital stay. Medical bills add up quickly, and you'll be glad that you planned for that.

FOR THOSE YOU CARE ABOUT

Life insurance is not as much for you as it is for your loved ones. If you have loved ones, you'll want to be sure they're cared for in the event of your death. And life insurance is much easier and less expensive to get if you buy it when you're young and still healthy.

INSURING A SMALL BUSINESS

Electrician insurance is basically small business insurance that encompasses factors such as liability, property, and business interruption insurance. Those first two parts have to do with something happening because of the work you've been a part of. For example, if faulty wiring causes a fire, you'd be liable for any medical bills, property losses, and other settlements and judgments.

Of course, no one wants to think they'd be responsible for anything like that. But humans make mistakes, and things can happen, so it's important to be covered in case they do. Business interruption insurance covers you if you need to shut down for a period. For example, if all your tools and your work truck are stolen, you might need to shut down to rebuild your inventory and purchase or lease a new vehicle. Business interruption insurance can cover the costs associated with this.

INSURANCE FOR INJURIES AND VEHICLES

Workers' compensation covers you and your employees if you or they are injured on the job. A person injured on the job may need specialized medical care not covered under their health plan. Workers' comp, as it's often called, can cover that.

Finally, if you have a vehicle or fleet of vehicles you use to travel to jobsites, you'll need commercial auto insurance.

Try not to be overwhelmed by discussion of insurances. They're just a fact of life in nearly every job.

CHAPTER 2

Getting Started

So, you've read through Chapter 1, and based on what you've learned, you may be even more certain that a career as an electrician is appealing. Now let's look at what you need to do to get there and examine some of the different areas in the field that might interest you.

DETERMINE WHAT TRAINING YOU NEED

You'll need a high school diploma or GED for all the jobs that we'll discuss in this book. A good foundation in math is also a requirement, because electricians use elements of algebra, geometry, and trigonometry in their work. It helps to be a critical thinker, too, since being an electrician involves a lot of problem-solving.

There are three main paths you can take to become an electrician after you finish high school:

- Attend trade school
- Attend community college
- Find an apprenticeship

Throughout the book, we'll explain what training and qualifications you need for different roles and how to get into the jobs.

You'll learn a lot on the job as an electrician, but you'll also need some basic skills and strengths, including basic math and critical-thinking skills.

Work to get your high school diploma or GED. Almost all trade schools will require you to have these important qualifications.

TRADE SCHOOL

Trade schools are for-profit organizations that offer specialized training in fields such as electrical work. They offer a range of classes, and if you select a good trade school, you'll get a solid base of training in the electrical field.

Some trade schools offer job placement services when you complete their program, and all claim they will prepare you to pass the necessary licensing exams. You'll need an apprenticeship after you finish trade school, so those placement services can be useful.

Trade school to become an electrician typically lasts anywhere from nine months to two years, depending on the program. There are trade schools all over the country, so you can search in your area to find one that seems like a good fit for your needs. Trade school costs vary widely, so be sure to evaluate the costs of various programs against what you'll learn.

One important consideration is to make sure the trade school you settle on is accredited. This is proof that the school you're attending will prepare you for a job in the field.

COMMUNITY COLLEGE

If you don't have a good trade school near you or if you feel trade school is too costly, community college is another option. If you have a community college in your area, search their academic programs and see whether they offer a program in becoming an electrician. Some offer a two-year associate's degree in the field, with many courses related to different careers within the electrical industry, and some offer a certificate program. Either way, you'll be poised to move on to an apprenticeship after your training at the community college.

Another important factor is that community college is typically quite affordable, with some states even offering free community college tuition to students for a certain period, such as the first year.

If you can, find people who have gone the trade school route, the community college route, and the apprenticeship route and talk to them about their experiences.

HANDS-ON TRAINING OR CLASSROOM-BASED LEARNING?

Some electricians have reported that trade school provides a lot more hands-on learning (whereas community college is typically more classroom based), but that is dependent on the program. If you can, talk to people who've done the programs you're considering and get their feedback on how they felt about the training. Did they feel they had enough hands-on learning? Are there ways they felt the program could be improved?

Talk to people at the community college admissions office and the dean or department chair as well. Find out whether the community college offers job placement services, as a trade school may.

In either trade school or community college, job-placement services can be a huge benefit. Even if you ultimately intend to open your own business, you'll need an apprenticeship, and placement services can help you find one.

You'll need a high school diploma or GED to enroll in a community college program.

APPRENTICESHIPS

Whether you attend trade school, community college, or neither, you'll need an apprenticeship. In an apprentice program, you train under an experienced professional in the field. Electrician apprenticeships typically last for several years and are paid—though the pay is on the lower side since you're still learning the trade. You must complete around 8,000 hours as an apprentice, so the exact number of years it will take you to complete an apprenticeship depends on how many hours a week you work. It's also important to note that if you attended trade school, that may count toward some of your required apprenticeship hours. You'll need to check with your specific apprenticeship. The same is true if you acquired electrician training in the military (which we'll discuss in a later chapter). Check with your apprenticeship to see whether the hours can count.

WHICH ROUTE?

Whether to choose trade school, community college, or apprenticeship is a personal decision. Only you know which road would be best for your situation. Talk to electricians in your area if you can and see what they recommend. There may be a great trade school or community college near you where you can learn the electrical trade at a reasonable cost. Or there may be a local electrical company that offers great apprenticeships. Talking to people in the field is a great way to narrow down the best option for you.

Remember that with all these options, you'll have to pass the certification tests required by your state or local area. Also bear in mind that some of those certification tests require you to have a certain amount of classroom experience. So when deciding which path you want to take, think about which one will best prepare you for the tests you will need to take.

Typically, much of your apprenticeship will be done in the field—you'll learn on the job under supervision.

GET LICENSED!

You must have an electrician license to be able to work as an electrician. In most states, licensing is handled at the state level. However, there are a few states with different municipalities that handle licensing. Check with your state to see what is applicable. (For example, the state of Arizona doesn't have licensing requirements; they are handled at local levels of government.)

Regardless of where you are and who is handling the licensing in that area, you will need a license. And regardless of where you are, the licensing will require you to have a thorough knowledge of the National Electric Code (NEC).

Different states and municipalities also have different types of electrician licenses. Many of them have apprentice, journeyman, and master electrician licenses. Some have others, too. Idaho, for example, has all three of the above licenses but also has an electrical contractor license. Each of the licenses builds on the previous one. For example, Oregon offers three licenses: journeyman, supervising, and electrical contractor. To earn your journeyman license, you must pass the exam. You must also have at least 8,000 hours of work experience (as an apprentice) and 576 hours of classroom training. To earn your supervising license, you must have at least 8,000 hours of experience as a journeyman and pass the exam. To earn your electrical contractor license, you must be or employ a general supervising electrician.

As you can see, a lot goes into getting your license. Carefully check the licensing requirements for the state where you think you'll be working to get an idea of what you will need to do when you reach the point of employment.

Licensing requirements will vary based on the state in which you live. You'll want to research what type of licenses you'll need to practice in your area.

However your journey to becoming an electrician unfolds, you'll ultimately need to work your way up. Electricians have very specific requirements they have to meet to progress to the next level in the field.

WORKING YOUR WAY UP

There are several levels you can achieve in your quest to become an electrician. Apprentice electricians work at an entry-level position under a more experienced electrician. They're still learning the trade. Generally, around 8,000 hours of work as an apprentice electrician are required before you can move up to journeyman. Journeyman electricians have finished their apprenticeship, passed a licensing exam to become a journeyman, and can work independently. Finally, master electricians have worked as journeymen for several hours (typically about 4,000). They have acquired even more experience and have passed a licensing exam. Master electricians have a wide breadth of knowledge of the electrical industry and often supervise other electricians. They also often design electrical systems and are in charge of pulling permits for projects from the local authority.

You'll need to be at least 18 to get a license to be an apprentice electrician, but you can start learning the field before you turn 18.

FINISHING HIGH SCHOOL

Now you have a good idea of what's involved in becoming an electrician, and the decisions you need to make about training. Obviously, some of these decisions don't need to be made immediately, as they pertain to your future work. But in the meantime, keep working toward your high school diploma. It is the key to almost any practical field.

You generally must be 18 years old to get a license to be an apprentice electrician. So it makes sense to finish your high school diploma from that standpoint as well. There's no point in skipping your high school diploma if you can't start working until 18, and we cannot emphasize enough that making the decision to get your diploma is a smart one.

GETTING A HEAD START

However, if you're set on getting a jump on your career as an electrician before you turn 18, you can explore whether there are vocational, or vo-tech, high schools in your area. Sometimes, there are vo-tech programs through the high school you're already attending, and sometimes, they're housed at a different campus. There are also some hybrid programs that allow you to attend regular high school classes for part of the day and then go to a vocational training center for another part of the day. You can check with your school guidance counselor to see whether any such programs are available in your area.

JOINING A UNION

You may have heard of unions but do not really know what they do or why they're important. You aren't required to join a union, but in many industries it's smart to consider it.

Electricians can work for union and non-union employers, and there's no way to say whether one is better than the other. It depends on the leadership and work environment in any given shop. However, in general, being part of a union means you have support if you need it. For example, you may at some point feel you have been unjustly terminated from your job. If you belong to a union, they can represent you when you speak to the company about your claim of wrongful termination.

In addition, electricians who are union members usually earn higher wages and have access to insurance and retirement plans. Some non-union shops may also offer insurance or retirement plans, but the quality of those plans may vary.

The downside to joining a union is that you must pay dues. These are usually taken directly out of your paycheck, and they typically aren't very high. You can check into the union in your area to find out what the dues will be, when you reach that point. However, it's still a budget consideration that you'll want to think about.

There are several different unions for electricians, but one large one is the International Brotherhood of Electrical Workers (IBEW). They are active in the United States and Canada, and they represent about 820,000 electricians.

If you ever run into problems while working as an electrician, you'll be glad to have the support of a union.

BUSTING MYTHS: NOT JUST FOR MEN

Women who work as electricians are helping to break down outdated stereotypes and are encouraging other women to enter the field.

Historically, the electrical industry has been heavily male-dominated. As recently as 2024, sources show that males made up more than 97 percent of electricians in the United States. Exact numbers are difficult to determine because different surveys have different data-collection methods. Either way, men make up most of the electrical industry.

WHERE ARE THE WOMEN?

It's difficult to say exactly why there are so few females currently working as electricians, but most people in the field say it is because of the difficult physical nature of the work as well as sexist attitudes within the industry. It is true that electricians must often lift or move heavy objects and wear heavy gear, which can be taxing. However, strength isn't necessarily dependent on gender. There are plenty of women who are strong enough to handle the physical demands of the job, and can do so capably.

BREAKING DOWN THE BARRIERS

Michele Robinson is a journeyman electrician in Milwaukee. She is also a board member of EmpowHER. This is a Milwaukee organization dedicated to supporting women in the trades. Robinson cites the isolation women experience in the industry. She comments that women can go a decade without seeing another female electrician on the job. As part of EmpowHER, Robinson has a goal to partner with local contractors on a training program that will help retain, or keep in work, female workers. Low retention has also been an issue in the trade. When women leave the field, those women are not necessarily replaced by other female electricians. That keeps the overall number of females in the trade on the low side.

BEATING THE STEREOTYPES

Brittley Richards is another journeyman plumber in the Milwaukee area who is helping break down the barriers. In fact, as a biracial woman in the field, Richards is breaking stereotypes in more ways than one. Richards' dream in life was to study dance performance—quite different from pursuing a career as an electrician! But her grandfather advised her to pursue a trade instead. He pointed out that dancers have a limited time span in which they can pursue that career. However, a person in the trades can work until retirement. Richards also had an advantage—as a regular dancer, she was strong. That helped her defeat the idea that women aren't strong enough to work in a trade such as electrical work.

COMPANIES CAN HELP TOO

Richards has done some of her work with Hurt Electric. The company has put in place a flexible start time for employees to enable caregivers (who are often female) to drop off children at school or daycare. Jean Hurt-Taylor, also a female journeyman electrician, hopes that similar support by companies will lead to an increase in female tradespeople. She hopes that at least 30 percent of electricians will be female by 2050.

JUST AS CAPABLE

"If you are female and really want to be an electrician, there is no reason why you can't do the job. Women are just as capable as men. We can learn the skills needed for the role, and carry out the job to high standards. If you want to pursue this career, go for it!"

CHAPTER 3

Different Jobs and Different Environments

In this chapter, we'll discuss the many different work environments you may have as an electrician. The term "work environment" describes the physical space, working conditions, and general approach that is part of a job. Work environment impacts how we feel at work and whether we enjoy our job, so it's an important consideration as you think about your future career. As an electrician, you'll have several different options for work environment, so you're sure to find one that suits you.

The four main types of work environments include those for:

- Outside linemen
- Inside wiremen
- Installation technicians
- Residential wiremen

OUTSIDE LINEMAN

Outside linemen work, as you would expect, outside. They are responsible for the power lines that are strung across cities and towns throughout the United States. Depending on where the job is, they may work in difficult weather conditions. Heavy snow and wind can damage power lines, and when that happens, it's the outside lineman's job to fix the problem.

QUALIFICATIONS AND TRAINING

Being a lineman is one of the more physically demanding jobs in the electrical field, so to take on this role you must be in good physical shape. You also must have extensive safety training. As a lineman, much of your time will be spent working on high-tension, high-voltage lines that can be hundreds of feet above the ground.

NOTE FOR GIRLS: DON'T BE PUT OFF BY THE TERMINOLOGY

The current lack of women in the electrical industry probably isn't helped by the terms used to describe different roles within the industry. For example, lineperson would be a better name for the job of lineman, since both men and women can do the job. But it's been lineman for so long that it's unlikely to change anytime soon—such changes can be very slow. You'll notice other similar terms in these job descriptions. They don't represent a requirement that someone must be male to perform the job—they simply are the names that currently exist. So if you're searching for a job in the field, bear in mind that you'll likely be searching by those terms.

Like any electrician, an outside lineman must be licensed as an apprentice to get started. As an apprentice, you'll most likely start as a groundman. When you've achieved the required number of hours to become a journeyman and you've successfully completed the certification exam, you'll be able to move on as a lineman.

You'll need a high school diploma or GED, a valid driver's license, and a clean background check.

Outside linemen make sure that power gets from generation facilities to end users. The number of users are likely to be high, too. Just one generation facility serves many customers—residential, business, and industrial.

WHAT'S THE PAY?

The median annual salary for linemen in the United States is just under $80,000. Keep in mind that in the apprentice phase, you'll make a lot less than that. But as you can see, once you work your way up, this can be a lucrative part of the industry to work in.

INSIDE WIREMAN

As an inside wireman, you'll work on the electrical wiring and power distribution in a client's premises. That is typically a commercial or industrial building. You will then connect that wiring to the external power source—the high-voltage lines that serve the building. You might need to install conduit through which wires are run. You might also install lighting fixtures and electrical outlets. You could be required to perform inspections and carry out maintenance on electrical control panels, electrical motors and equipment, and alarm systems.

QUALIFICATIONS AND TRAINING

Like any electrician, you'll need to be a licensed apprentice to get started. You may have completed a trade school or community college program. Alternatively, you may have started a dedicated apprenticeship program that includes hands-on training as well as classroom instruction.

A high school diploma or GED is needed, a valid driver's license, and a clean background check.

If working inside suits you more than being outside, you might look into becoming an inside wireman.

Another job that takes place mostly indoors is installation technician.

WHAT'S THE PAY?

While it varies greatly based on location and who you're working for (union shops generally pay more than non-union), in general the average annual salary for an inside wireman working in the United States is around $60,000.

INSTALLATION TECHNICIAN

Installation technicians typically work inside, since their job duties include installing the low-voltage wiring that is used for data, video, and voice outlets. However, that doesn't mean they escape challenging working conditions in terms of temperature. As an installation tech, you are likely to often work in a brand-new construction. It may or may not have had the HVAC (heating, ventilation, and air conditioning) installed. For that reason, you may work in very hot or very cold environments, even when inside.

QUALIFICATIONS AND TRAINING

Like any electrician, to work as an installation technician you will need to be a licensed apprentice to get started. You may have completed a trade school or community college program. Alternatively, you may have started a dedicated apprenticeship program that includes hands-on training as well as classroom instruction.

You will need a high school diploma or GED, a valid driver's license, and a clean background check.

WHAT'S THE PAY?

As for an inside wireman, the pay for an installation technician varies greatly based on location. The pay also depends on the organization you're working for—union shops generally pay more than non-union shops. In general, you can expect the average annual salary for an installation technician to be similar to that of an inside wireman.

With no shortage of buildings being built, there's plenty of work for both residential and commercial electricians.

RESIDENTIAL WIREMAN

Residential wiremen perform similar tasks to those of inside wiremen. In this role, you would connect a client's equipment to the external power source. However, you would work in personal residences only, whereas inside wiremen typically work in commercial or industrial buildings. In your work on people's homes, you might install security systems, fire alarm systems, energy-management systems, and more.

QUALIFICATIONS AND TRAINING

Like other electricians, you'll need to be a licensed apprentice to get started. You may have completed a trade school or community college program, or you may have started a dedicated apprenticeship program that includes hands-on training as well as classroom instruction.

A high school diploma or GED is needed, a valid driver's license, and a clean background check.

WHAT'S THE PAY?

Once again, pay varies based on what part of the country you work in and the organizations you're working for. And of course, union shops will typically pay employees more than non-union shops. However, in general, the average annual salary that can be expected if working as a residential wireman is around $66,000 per year.

HAVE YOU GOT WHAT IT TAKES?

Are you wondering if you've got what it takes to be an electrician? If so, here are six key skills that help contribute to a successful career in the field:

- **Strong communication skills:** You'll need to communicate with customers and/or fellow contractors, so good communication skills are vital.
- **Technical know-how:** You must have good technical knowledge both to read blueprints and to understand circuits and wiring.
- **Good problem-solving skills:** A lot of electrical work involves solving problems. For that reason, being able to analyze an issue and troubleshoot the problem is an essential skill for an electrician.
- **Safety awareness:** There is a level of danger in being an electrician. You will be working with live wires, and there is the potential for being shocked or electrocuted if you are not taking proper precautions. Safety awareness is key.
- **Good time management:** As with any trade in the construction area, you'll need good time-management skills. If you're working on new construction or remodels, you'll be part of a team of individuals working toward a common goal. If you don't get your part done on time, it affects the next person down the line in your team.

  And if you're an electrician troubleshooting problems in customers' homes or businesses, the more efficiently you get your job done, the quicker you can move on to the next one. And completing more jobs means you earn more too.
- **Adaptability:** Electrical work is always changing, particularly in the current age of renewable energy sources and energy-saving plans. The best electricians are open to change and open to using new technologies as they arise.

CAREER OPPORTUNITIES

"Once you've completed your training, there are lots of different lines of work you can go into, from commercial to industrial or residential. There are plenty of options for everyone."

CHAPTER 4

Specialized Jobs for Electricians

In the previous chapter, we discussed four major types of work environments for electricians. However, within those work environments you can also explore more specialized areas of the electrical industry. In this next chapter, we'll look at some of those more specialized jobs.

WORKING AS A MAINTENANCE ELECTRICIAN

Maintenance electricians perform routine maintenance on electrical systems, often in a non-residential building as opposed to a home. However, some work in individual homes if they are employed by an organization such as a property management company.

Maintenance electricians keep things running smoothly.

WORKING YOUR WAY UP

When you explore the field of electrician jobs, you'll often see the terms residential, commercial, and industrial pop up. Residential typically involves work carried out in private homes or individual apartments or condos. Commercial and industrial are less well known. Both involve work on non-home environments. However, the difference is that industrial electricians work on the electrical systems in factories, industrial plants, and similar sites. Commercial electricians work on the electrical systems in sites such as stores, retail centers, offices, and other places of business.

This type of organization may provide management for entire apartment or housing complexes. In this role, you would regularly inspect the system using various diagnostic tools that help figure out any potential problems. You would then perform repairs and upgrades as needed to keep the system running smoothly. Parts such as breakers, switches, and even general wiring can wear out over time or can become damaged due to environmental conditions or problems such as being gnawed by rats or mice, so maintenance electricians solve those issues.

QUALIFICATIONS AND TRAINING

To be a maintenance electrician, you'll need a high school diploma or GED. You'll also need at least a journeyman license, so you must have completed your apprenticeship. (Of course, you might do your apprenticeship under a maintenance electrician, so that's one way you can get a foot in the door.) You'll need a valid driver's license, a clean background check, and a good knowledge of the NEC.

WHAT'S THE PAY?

Pay varies widely depending on who you work for and what part of the country you're in. However, the average annual salary for a maintenance electrician in the United States is around $57,000 per year.

EINSTEIN AND ELECTRICITY

Albert Einstein is best known as a Nobel Prize-winning physicist who developed the Theory of Relativity. However, Einstein worked for his father's electrician business when he was young. One of his first jobs involved running electric lights to the first Oktoberfest in Munich, Germany. The lights were lit by a steam generator, and Einstein then had to walk around the fair to ensure that all the lights were working. Design, installation, inspection, and maintenance—all in one job for the young Einstein!

There are plenty of jobs in the electrical field, so if you find that you are not enjoying one, you can switch to another.

THE ROLE OF CONSTRUCTION ELECTRICIAN

Construction electricians typically work on new construction. That can be construction of homes, buildings, or industrial facilities. In construction, electricians are generally involved in designing, planning, and installing the wiring and electrical systems for the new construction in question. These systems don't just involve plugs for appliances and the wiring of them. They can involve heating, cooling, communication, power, and lighting too.

QUALIFICATIONS AND TRAINING

To work as a construction electrician, you'll need a high school diploma or GED. You'll also need at least a journeyman license, so you must have completed your apprenticeship. You can also do your apprenticeship under a construction electrician. You'll need a valid driver's license, a clean background check, and knowledge of both the NEC and the building codes for your area.

WHAT'S THE PAY?

The average annual salary for a construction electrician working in the United States is around $60,000 per year.

Working on a new construction is exciting. You are at the cutting edge of its development.

ELECTRICAL DESIGNER

As an electrical designer, it would be your job to design the electrical systems for residential, commercial, or industrial projects. You would need to ensure that the designs meet local safety codes, and make sure they don't conflict with other systems installed in the building, such as plumbing or HVAC systems. Your job would be to create the designs and then work with other contractors and electricians to evaluate whether the designs are feasible for each project. At higher levels, electrical designers may also work on plans for high-voltage systems, such as when transmission lines need to be extended to a new development.

QUALIFICATIONS AND TRAINING

Electrical designers take a somewhat different path from other professionals we've looked at so far in the electrical field. As with any of the other careers in the industry, you'll need a high school diploma or GED. However, instead of going to trade school or community college for basic electrician training, you'll need to get at least an associate's degree in electrical design or engineering technology. (Many electrical design jobs will require a four-year degree, but not all, and you may be able to use relevant experience in the field to offset the lack of a bachelor's degree if you don't have one.) You'll also need a strong knowledge of computer-aided design (CAD) software to carry out the job.

You'll need a valid driver's license, a clean background check, and a good knowledge of the NEC and building codes for your area.

VARIED WORK

"Working in construction electricity is really interesting. Every day brings something new. It's never boring."

Becoming an electrical designer requires some schooling, but it's a great career option for people with strong design skills.

WHAT'S THE PAY?

Pay for an electrical designer varies and is dependent on whether you've completed a four-year degree. However, the average annual salary for a construction electrician in the United States is around $65,000 per year. People who have gained their full bachelor's degree in electrical engineering will earn even more than that.

A WORLD OF OPPORTUNITY

As you can see, there are many outside-the-box opportunities for people interested in a career in electrical work. Hopefully these few options have given you some exciting ideas as you consider your future career as an electrician. Your career options really are wide open in the electrical industry, which gives you a lot of room to find the fit that is right for you.

In the next chapter, we'll look at some even more specialized jobs in the electrical industry. So much of our modern world relies on electricity that there really is no end to the number of jobs and areas of the field you can work in.

Nikola Tesla (see opposite) was an inspirational scientist who helped shape our use of electricity.

JOB SECURITY

"You can always find a job as an electrician. Everyone needs electricians, and there aren't enough of us. I've never been out of work. There has always been a demand for electricians, and that demand is continually growing."

THE INSPIRATIONAL NIKOLA TESLA

Thomas Edison and Benjamin Franklin are well known for their contributions to the study and use of electricity in the United States. However, an incredibly influential person in the field doesn't always get as much recognition: Serbian-American inventor Nikola Tesla.

Tesla discovered technologies that are the basis of the modern alternating current (AC) electrical supply system. In short, alternating current allows electricity to be efficiently transmitted through high-voltage lines. It also allows power to be changed to lower voltage for use in a home or office building, for example.

Tesla worked with Thomas Edison for a time. In fact, the two men were reported to be at odds because Tesla's alternating current was a competing technology to Edison's direct current (DC). There are uses for both alternating and direct current, so there's not a definitive answer as to which technology is better—despite the so-called "War of the Currents" that occurred between Tesla and Edison. And in case you're wondering, yes, the Tesla automobile was named after Nikola Tesla. Perhaps Elon Musk, creator of Tesla, is on Team Tesla in the War of the Currents!

Elon Musk has made innovative use of electrical technology to revolutionize the electric vehicle (EV) industry.

CHAPTER 5

Alternative Roles for Electricians

We've talked about the different work environments in the electrical field as well as some of the more common jobs in the industry. But there are many more jobs available for people who are interested in working in the electrical trade. This chapter will highlight a few more you might not have thought of, and which could be a fit for you.

THE MILITARY ALSO NEEDS ELECTRICIANS

You may not have considered enlisting in the military, but that is another way you can get training and work as an electrician. All four major branches of the military (army, navy, air force, and marines) use electricians. Though the job titles vary, the training and job duties are similar across the four.

WHAT YOU'LL LEARN

Electricians in the military install, repair, and maintain electrical systems and equipment, such as service panels and switches. They read and interpret blueprints as needed to perform their job, and use testing equipment to make sure all circuits are working properly. And there are lineman-type jobs in the military as well. These electricians install, maintain, test, and repair overhead and underground power distribution systems.

Military electricians work on many different electrical systems and components, including transformers, capacitor banks, breakers, and fuses.

If you choose to do your electrical training through the military, not only will it be free, but you will also be paid to train.

Like electricians in the civilian world, electricians in the military also prepare cost estimates for jobs and ensure that all jobs are completed in line with the relevant codes. Similarly, military electricians may also work indoors or outdoors.

WHAT YOU'LL GET

When you enlist in the military, you must go through basic training. That involves rigorous physical training, weapons training, military life and customs training, and tactical and survival skills training. Aspiring electricians in the military also go through specific classroom and hands-on training that includes training on installation and the repair of electrical wiring systems. It also covers the basics of electricity and electronics, electrical circuit troubleshooting and maintenance, and safety essentials. Another part of the education is techniques for wiring various components of electrical systems, such as junction boxes, switches, and outlets.

WHAT'S THE PAY?

You are paid for your military services, and typically the military pays above the federal minimum wage. You also get health insurance, allowances for food, clothing, and housing, and education benefits. If you decide you enjoy the military life and you stay enlisted for longer than the minimum enlistment period, the retirement benefits can be quite good. Some people who serve in the military choose to serve for 20 years so they can retire with a good pension. They retire from the military in their late thirties and then take a civilian job, where they earn regular pay plus a significant military pension. Essentially, they get double pay for the remainder of their working days.

A GREAT START

"Working in the military helped me gain a really wide range of skills, from general skills to specific electrical skills."

A HELPING HAND WITH HIRING

It's worth noting that your military training and work as an electrician may count toward your apprenticeship hours when you finish your military service and enter the civilian working world. And military training is generally looked upon well. That means you'll have a good chance of being hired for a position in the civilian world.

WHAT YOU NEED

If you want to pursue your electrician training in the military, you'll need to be at least 17 years old with parental consent. You must be 18 without parental consent. You must also be a US citizen or permanent resident with a valid Green Card. You'll also need a high school diploma or GED—as is the case for virtually all jobs in the electrician world. Note that the military prefers a high school diploma—they may accept a GED, but they prefer a high school diploma. You'll need to pass a physical fitness exam, and you'll need to pass a background check.

You'll also need a qualifying score on the Armed Services Vocational Aptitude Battery (ASVAB). So if you're interested in enlisting in the military, talk to a military recruiter and they will help you prepare to take the required ASVAB.

You'll have to pass the ASVAB to get an electrician job in the military. But if you do, there are plenty of opportunities to get training in different types of electrical work. And when you leave the military, you'll leave with those skills.

ENLISTING IS SERIOUS BUSINESS

Joining the military to start your electrician career might sound very appealing. You get paid, there are a lot of extra benefits offered, and you get quality training to set you up in your career. However, joining the military is a major commitment and not to be taken lightly. When you enlist in the military, you are committing to serve your country. It is against the law to "quit." So once you're in, you're in—unless you have a very compelling reason to leave. In that case you might be granted an honorable discharge.

The other important point about being in the military is that when you commit to serve your country, you commit to go where they need you to go and do what they need you to do. If the United States were to go to war while you were enlisted, you could very well find yourself on the front lines. And even during peace time, military life typically comes with many moves. So if you like to settle in one place and not move around a lot, the military life may not be for you.

AVIATION ELECTRICIAN

One interesting area of the electrical field is aviation electronics. Aviation electricians do the same types of work as other electricians, but they work specifically on airplanes. In this role you would install, maintain, test, and repair the planes' electronic systems, electrical equipment, and components. You'd work on the planes' communication devices, navigation systems, and radar equipment. It would be your responsibility to perform tests on electronics and wiring to ensure safety for passengers and crew. You'd then fix any problems found, and also do routine maintenance to ensure that the plane is safe.

If planes and aircraft are your passion, have you thought about a career as an aviation electrician?

QUALIFICATIONS AND TRAINING

Unlike many of the electrician jobs we've discussed, to be an aviation electrician you also need to be licensed by the Federal Aviation Administration (FAA) in addition to all the normal requirements for an electrician job. To pass the exam for certification, it's highly recommended that you spend at least some of your apprenticeship hours working on aircraft.

Although it's not required, many people who become aviation electricians have a two-year associate's degree in electrical technology, which you can typically earn at a community college. There are also FAA-approved programs in electronics you can explore if you're interested.

WHAT'S THE PAY?

Aviation electricians typically make more than residential electricians, with the median annual salary about $75,000 per year.

WORKING AS A MARINE ELECTRICIAN

Aviation electricians work on vessels bound for the sky, but marine electricians work on vessels bound for the water. They may work on boats in dry dock at a shipyard, staying on land, or they may work on a cruise ship crossing the ocean.

In this role, you would work on the wiring and electrical systems on any type of boat or ship. That would include installing and configuring generators and shore-power connections that deliver energy to boat systems. You'd also work on the wiring, electronics, motors, and pumps throughout the ship. You would work on many types of electrical circuits since boats use systems with different voltages for different components.

As you probably know, water and electricity is not a great combination. Water conducts electricity, which means it allows it to travel through it easily. That can quickly create a dangerous situation. As such, you'd spend a lot of time dealing with the issues caused by having water constantly around electrical systems. It would be your responsibility to ensure that high-voltage current doesn't escape into the water around a ship, which can pose a major danger to nearby swimmers or sea life. You'd also deal with low-voltage currents, which when combined with water can result in galvanic corrosion. This is a process in which two metals exposed to electric current in a conductive solution (water) quickly corrode.

Boats and watercraft also have numerous electrical systems that need to be maintained and repaired. Perhaps a career as a marine electrician could be a good fit for you?

QUALIFICATIONS AND TRAINING

The training to become a marine electrician is different from the training needed to become a residential or commercial electrician, particularly if you're working on vessels out at sea.

Marine electricians typically attend vocational programs at specialized maritime academies. There are also a few community college maritime programs on which you can earn a certificate in marine electrical systems. If you're planning to work on ships in dry dock, you may be able to go through the same training as any other electrician. But to work on a vessel when it's in water, you'll need to attend a specialized maritime academy or marine certificate program.

If you choose to be a marine electrician, you can work on boats in dry dock or out at sea.

To work on a vessel at sea, you may also need particular certifications. They include a Transportation Workers Identification Card (TWIC) or Standards of Training, Certification, and Watchkeeping (STCW) certification, depending on your job role and the vessel you'll be working on. Both certifications are issued by the Coast Guard and they cover safety at sea.

You'll likely also want to get your marine electrical certification in American Boat and Yacht Council (ABYC) standards. This is not required, but most ship and boat builders and service companies want their staff to be ABYC certified. If you have your ABYC certification before you apply for jobs in the industry, it's looked upon well by potential employers.

You'll also need the same state- or local-level licenses as any electrician in your area. So, for example, if your state requires apprentices to be licensed, you'll need your license to apprentice as a marine electrician.

WHAT'S THE PAY?

In general the average annual salary for a marine electrician is around $70,000 per year. That's more than the average annual salary for a residential or commercial electrician, so is well-paid indeed.

THE WORLD IS YOUR OYSTER

There really is unlimited potential with careers in the electrical field. There are so many to choose from, and there are some real gems. After we talk a little more about the future for electricians in the next chapter, you'll find a list of some more jobs in the electrical field that you might not have thought of.

CHAPTER 6

Your Career Future

When you're considering a career, it's crucial to think about the future and how that career may look in years to come. There are no absolutes as to what the future holds. However, you can look at the information available today and what that suggests about the future of the electrical industry.

LOOKING AHEAD

According to the BLS, job growth for electricians in the United States over the next decade is predicted to be 6 percent. That is double the average for all occupations in general. It used to be common for people to go into electrical as a trade. However, as you've learned, in recent years there has been a decline in the number of people pursuing trade occupations. This is good news for practical-minded people who want to work as electricians or in another trade. Less interest in trade jobs equals more opportunities for you!

The predicted job growth for electricians in the next decade is impressive. It could be a great time to enter this field.

NEW ENERGY

The continuing focus on "green" solutions and alternative energy sources is also good news for aspiring electricians. Homeowners are retrofitting their homes to make use of alternative energy sources and energy-efficient solutions. Electricians are needed to help with these conversions and installations. They install solar panels on homes and buildings, for example, or they switch gas furnaces to electric ones.

In addition, electricians are needed to link alternative energy sources to the power grid. For example, wind turbines capture energy. However, that energy then needs to be linked to the power grid to generate the electricity that is used for homes and buildings. And that's where electricians come in.

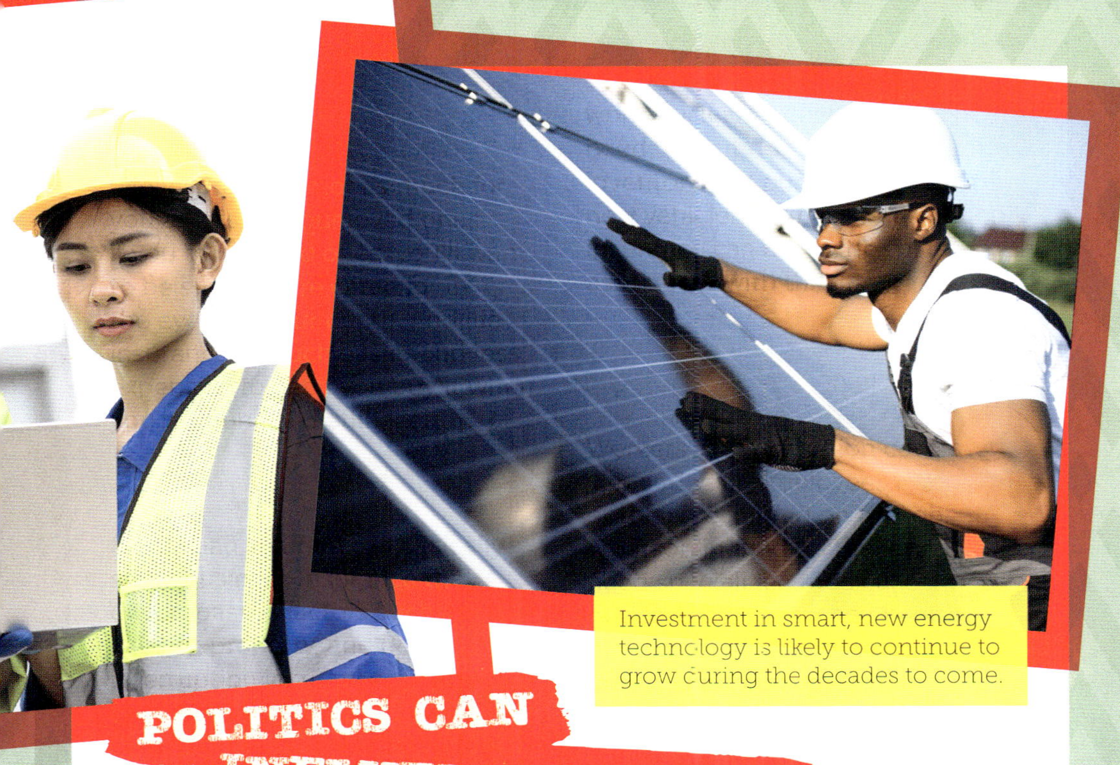

Investment in smart, new energy technology is likely to continue to grow during the decades to come.

POLITICS CAN INFLUENCE DEMAND

The BLS cautions that the need for electricians to help continue the conversion to more energy-efficient solutions and the use of alternative energy sources is dependent on government. The government creates plans such as tax credits and incentives to encourage people in certain areas. Those political plans can have a big impact. For example, the government might offer a big incentive for people to purchase EVs. In that instance, the demand for those vehicles goes up because consumers are willing to buy them. When the incentives expire, the demand for EVs goes down.

Changes in government provision are dependent on politics. Some political administrations value environmental causes. They put in place programs and incentives that prize eco-conscious solutions and alternative energy sources. Other political administrations have other priorities and don't put in place such programs. But keep in mind that political administrations change every four to eight years. That means if there's a slow period in terms of the demand for electricians who can install solar panels, for example, you need only wait until the next political administration, and the demand will likely pick up again.

SOLAR AND WIND ENERGY

There are numerous alternative energy sources, but two common ones are solar and wind energy. Solar is particularly common in residential electrics because homeowners can install solar panels on their roofs and pull in electricity. It's a solution that doesn't require much space and is commonly done.

Wind power is a little less common than solar power in the residential world. That is because many people don't have room for a wind turbine in their yard. However, it's still a very common alternative energy source in the bigger pictures, and you may have seen fields of wind turbines while traveling.

Electricians are needed to wire solar panels, wind turbines, and the battery storage systems that go along with them. The panels and turbines capture energy from the sun and wind, respectively. However, that energy needs to be stored and then distributed.

The use of wind power to generate electricity has created a lot of new jobs in the electrical field in recent years.

THE POWER GRID

The power grid is an enormous storage system that transports electricity to homes and businesses and factories. But how does that electricity get to the grid? Today, it comes from many sources. They include green energy such as solar panels, wind turbines, and hydropower and geothermal power.

Because the grid gets its energy from multiple sources, it needs to be modernized for two-way flow. It used to be the case that electricity from the grid flowed in just one direction: from power plants to consumers. Today, it needs to flow two ways. It needs to take in energy from the multiple renewable energy sources. It then needs to send that energy (electricity) back out to consumers. It works like a give and take. If you have solar panels on your house, it's likely the energy you capture from the sun doesn't just power your house. Instead, it goes back into the grid so the excess can also power other homes.

Solar power has also created many new jobs in the electrical sector—and that job growth is unlikely to reverse.

Electricians are needed to help modernize the grid for the two-way energy flow that we now require. This is a more complicated system than the traditional one-way flow. For that reason, it's likely that electricians will be needed for this important work for a long time. Even when modernization is complete, maintenance and updates will be needed.

"SMART" DEVICES

Electrical systems are becoming "smarter." That is because they have inbuilt monitoring to detect problems and ensure maximum efficiency. Such systems require electricians to monitor the sensors and data and to repair and maintain the systems where needed.

MOVING FORWARD

As you can see, the future is very promising for electricians. There should be plenty of work, and smart electricians will make sure to keep up to date on the latest developments and technologies to position them well in the industry. The world of electrics is constantly changing and growing, so for anyone interested in this practical career, the future is very bright!

ON-THE-JOB TRAINING

"I learned as I earned. That was one of the great things about the job. I didn't come through my training with a lot of debt, like some of my friends who did a degree. I went straight into paid work."

MORE PRACTICAL CAREERS

You can enjoy many different jobs in the electrical industry. We've picked out some of them, but there are many others to choose from too, so if none of the jobs on the following pages fit your dream career, turn to pages 62–63. There you'll find links to sites at which you can research even more jobs in the electrical industry.

WIND TURBINE ELECTRICIAN

Wind turbine electricians help install new wind turbines. They also inspect and troubleshoot the electrical systems and wiring on wind turbines. They then perform routine maintenance and repairs as needed. They service the wiring and electrical systems on underground transmission systems. The part of the wind turbine that generates electricity is called the nacelle. Wind turbine electricians inspect, maintain, and repair the electrical equipment within the nacelle.

QUALIFICATIONS AND TRAINING

People interested in becoming a wind turbine electrician must have a high school diploma or GED. They must be licensed according to the rules of their state or municipality.

In general, wind turbine electricians should have training through a trade school or community college. However, it is also possible to simply start as an apprentice electrician in general and be hired as a wind turbine electrician after you have at least part of your apprentice training done. (The IBEW, one of the main unions for electrical workers, for example, has created a training program to help electricians train for wind turbine work.)

Before becoming a journeyman and working without supervision on turbines, wind turbine electricians must have gained a certain number of hours under instruction. They must have 144 hours of technical instruction. They also need to have had 2,000 hours of hands-on training in electrical, safety, and mechanical systems maintenance.

The BLS projects that in the next 10 years, job growth for this profession will be 22 percent. That is far higher than the expected job growth of 3 percent across all occupations.

Salaries vary for wind turbine technicians based on location and other factors, but the BLS reports that the average annual salary in 2023 was $61,860.

SOLAR PHOTOVOLTAICS INSTALLER

Solar power is becoming increasingly common in all sectors, including residential. In California, all new homes must be built with solar panels. So far, California is the only state to require this, but it's likely that others will eventually follow. And even in states without this requirement, many homeowners and business owners are choosing to install solar panels to help cut down on their energy costs and to contribute to a greener future. As such, solar photovoltaics (PV) installers will be in great demand in coming years.

Solar PV installers put in place and maintain rooftop PV systems. They assess a customer's roof to ensure that it's a good fit for a solar panel. Roofs that are shaded most of the day are not good candidates, typically. Sun exposure is needed to gather energy from the sun. After inspection, installers measure, cut, and assemble the support structure needed for the solar panels. They install the panels according to local building codes, and connect the panels to the electrical system. They activate, test, and maintain the PV systems as well.

QUALIFICATIONS AND TRAINING

PV installers need a high school diploma or GED. They also typically take courses at a trade school or community college to learn about solar panel installation. Online courses are also sometimes available. PV installers need hands-on training, which usually lasts for the first one to 12 months of their job. They may also complete an apprenticeship. Some states and municipalities require PV installers to be licensed, and you can check the requirements for your area.

Another consideration when planning your career will be to think about what jobs will be in your area. For example, some areas have more jobs in alternative energy fields than others, or you may find your area has a high number of automotive electrician jobs.

There are also two certifications for PV installers that can make you a good candidate for more jobs. They are offered through the Electronics Technicians Association (ETA), International (ETA), and the North American Board of Certified Energy Practitioners (NABCEP). While they are not required, they will open more job opportunities for you. That is because for some projects eligible for solar-related funding, all installers on the job must have these certifications.

WHAT'S THE PAY?

Salaries vary for PV installers based on location and other factors, but the average annual salary is around $50,000.

AUTOMOTIVE ELECTRICIAN

Automotive electricians work on the electrical systems and associated wiring in vehicles. These can include the ignition systems, air conditioning systems, and alarms. They also include sound systems, brakes, lights, and more. Automotive electricians install the wiring systems and diagnose any problems with the wiring and electrical components.

QUALIFICATIONS AND TRAINING

Those interested in a career as an automotive electrician need a high school diploma or GED. You'll need a basic understanding of vehicle engines, and you'll need an apprenticeship with an automotive electrician. You may also be able to get electrical training from a general auto repair program if you can't find a specific apprenticeship with an automotive electrician. You'll need a valid driver's license, too, because you'll be working on vehicles.

You may also require certifications, such as those offered through the National Institute for Automotive Service Excellence (ASE). Some employers require you to have your master electrician license, but others are willing to hire at the apprentice level or if you're a journeyman.

WHAT'S THE PAY?

How much you earn is dependent on a number of factors, including where you work and whether you're working in a union or non-union shop. However, the average annual salary is about $47,700.

SOMETHING FOR EVERYONE

"I was always interested in cars, but I didn't know how that would fit with my interest in electrics. I did some research and decided to go for being an automotive electrician. It has allowed me to combine both my interests. It's a great job."

WHAT'S NEXT? YOUR CAREER CHECKLIST

As you can see, there are many exciting career opportunities for electricians, and this area of practical work looks set to keep on expanding in the future. If you think you'd like to progress with a career as an electrician, let's look at some questions you need to ask and steps you need to take next.

QUESTIONS TO ASK ABOUT SCHOOLS AND COURSES

- Is the program accredited? (Whether you choose trade school or an apprenticeship through a community college, this is an important question. Accredited programs guarantee that you'll get a quality education. They are also more attractive to potential employers than unaccredited programs.)
- What types of training and classes are offered in your program?
- Do you offer specialty programs in different areas of the field?
- How rigorous is the program? (You need to know how much time to devote to your studies daily. Some people attend community college part time while they work, but some programs may require that you devote yourself to them full time.)
- How much hands-on training does your program allow, compared to classroom learning?
- What certifications can I expect to earn upon completion of your program?
- Do you offer job-placement services through your program?
- How much does your program cost, and is financial aid available?

QUESTIONS TO ASK ABOUT APPRENTICESHIPS

- How many hours a week can I expect to work? (You need a certain number of hours to finish an apprenticeship, so this is an important question.)
- What parts of the trade can I expect to learn in an apprenticeship with you? (There are many different angles to the electrical industry, so you want to make sure the apprenticeship in question offers what you're looking for.)
- Will your program help prepare me for licensing exams?
- What is the pay?

KEY QUESTIONS TO ASK WHEN BEING INTERVIEWED FOR A JOB

- Do you provide opportunities for continued learning?
- Do you pay for certification classes and tests?
- What is your benefits package? (This typically covers medical insurance, life insurance, vacation time or paid time off, and also retirement benefits. By asking this one question about benefits, you'll get the answer to several more questions at the same time, which is very useful.)
- Does this position require overtime often?
- What is the salary? (Don't forget to ask this all-important question!)

NAIL THAT INTERVIEW!

Being interviewed can feel stressful. But here are some great steps you can take to ensure your interview goes as well as possible.

- Dress for success! Wear clean, well-fitting clothes that are free from words or questionable graphics.
- Research the position and company. The more you know about who is interviewing you and what they do, the better placed you'll be to answer questions they may have.
- Prepare some questions to ask ahead of time. Almost every interview ends with the employer asking you whether you have any questions for them. Have a question or two ready.
- Thank the interviewer for their time.
- Follow up with a thank-you note by email or even text afterward.

GLOSSARY

accredítation a certification that a school has met a specific set of standards set by an external group that regulates such schools

apprenticeship a position in which a person works for lower wages while learning a trade from a skilled professional

Armed Services Vocational Aptitude Battery (ASVAB) a test given to military enlistees to determine their aptitude and help guide their placement in the military

artificial intelligence (AI) technology designed to imitate human thought

associate's degree a two-year degree awarded to students who have completed a particular course of study at a community college

bachelor's degree a degree awarded to students who have completed a particular four-year course of study at a college or university

basic training a period of training for all new military enlistees

benefits services provided by employers in addition to wages. May include benefits such as health insurance, life insurance, retirement packages, stock options, and paid time off work

biracial describes a person whose mother and father were of two different ethnic origins

blueprints guides, designs, and plans that help with construction

carbonized converted into a carbon

certification a designation that one has completed a course of study (and usually passed a test), and has acquired a certain body of knowledge required in a field

civilian a person who is not in the military

client a person you are completing work for

community college a college that offers various associate's degrees as well as courses that can transfer to a university if a student wishes to pursue a bachelor's degree

components parts of something

computer-aided design (CAD) the use of software to digitally create a design or schematic

conduit a channel through which something, such as electricity, flows

corrode wearing down a metal

corrosion the process of a metal becoming worn away

diagnostic a tool used to diagnose a problem, or figure out what is causing a problem

dry dock a dock drained of water that allows technicians and mechanics to inspect and repair a ship's hull

electrocuted experienced an electric shock

filament a thin, threadlike object used to conduct electricity

health insurance medical coverage to help a person pay medical bills for care or emergencies

incandescent light bulb a light bulb that produces light through the glow of a wire heated by an electric current

junction box a box that houses electrical connections

licenses certificates that show you are legally allowed to do a job

lucrative capable of producing much profit

marine related to the oceans

maritime relating to the oceans

Medicare a federal health insurance system for people over age 65 and some people with disabilities. Everyone must pay into Medicare through their employer taxes or through self-employment tax

myth a story told that many people believe but is not based on fact

nacelle a housing for the electrical systems of a wind turbine

National Electric Code (NEC) a common standard for the safe installation of electrical equipment and wiring in the United States

patent a government license that says an invention may be produced by only the patent holder for a specified period

renewable energy energy that can be replaced, such as energy from the sun, wind, water, or heat within Earth

retrofitting to install new parts or modify existing systems

robot a machine that can replicate human movements

self-employed working for oneself, not employed by another person or organization

self-employment tax a required tax for contractors or others who are self-employed. It covers Medicare and Social Security taxes that normally are taken out of one's paycheck by one's employer

sensor a device that detects something and responds to it

Social Security a government program that provides money to people who are retired or disabled

stereotypes oversimplified ideas about people based on their sex, background, or ethnic group

student loan a specific type of loan taken out by a person to attend college, university, or trade school

total compensation package the salary and benefits offered by an employer to an employee. It may include wages, insurance, stock options, bonuses, and more

trade school a school that offers training for a particular career

university an institute of higher learning where students can earn a bachelor's degree and often a master's degree or doctorate degree

vocational related to work, for example, a school offers classes to students to train them for a skilled job or a trade

workers' compensation a type of insurance that covers lost wages and medical costs for employees injured on a job

FIND OUT MORE

BOOKS

Mason, P.D. *Apprenticeship Career Planning for Teens: A Comprehensive Guide to Securing Apprenticeships in High Demand Industries Without Taking On Years Of College Debt.* SugarDog Publishing, 2023.

Mason, P.D. *Skilled Trade Career Planning for Teens: The Handbook Of Lucrative Skilled Trades & High Paying Occupations That Don't Require Expensive College Degrees.* SugarDog Publishing, 2023.

McCauley, Pamela. *Engineering for Teens: A Beginner's Book for Aspiring Engineers.* Callisto Teens, 2021.

WEBSITES

Bureau of Labor Statistics (BLS)

Take a look at the BLS website to find out more about the role and outlook for electricians:

www.bls.gov/ooh/construction-and-extraction/electricians.htm

Explore the Trades

Explore the Trades is a great site for those interested in the plumbing, HVAC, and electrical trades. It provides a wealth of information on many aspects of working in these trades:

www.explorethetrades.org

Exploring

Exploring is a site that offers information about a lot of different paths for your future. They have a dedicated portion for trades, but the entire site is worth looking around in case there are other areas you're thinking of pursuing. They have a training portal and an activity library, too:

www.exploring.org

Tradeswomen Inc.

This site was created as part of a support organization for the outreach, recruitment, retention, and leadership development for women interested in careers in the trades. It offers resources and information for females interested in pursuing trade careers:

www.tradeswomen.org

Publisher's note to educators and parents:

All the websites featured above have been carefully reviewed to ensure that they are suitable for students. However, many websites change often, and we cannot guarantee that a site's future contents will continue to meet our high standards of educational value. Please be advised that students should be closely monitored whenever they access the Internet.

INDEX

ABOUT THE AUTHOR

Cathleen Small has written many books for young people on a wide variety of topics. She hopes this book will show readers that there are many exciting job opportunities for people who are interested in working as an electrician, and that the information provided will help set them on their path toward a perfect practical career.